From Victim to Victor

From Victim to Victor

. . .

A Biblical Recipe for Turning Your Hurting into Healing

Yvonne Martinez

RPI Publishing, Inc.

Published by
Recovery Publications, Inc.
1201 Knoxville Street
San Diego, CA 92110-3718
(619) 275-1350

Library of Congress Cataloging-in-Publication Data
Martinez, Yvonne, 1949–
From victim to victor : a biblical guide for turning hurting into
healing / Yvonne Martinez. — 1st ed.
p.   cm.
Includes bibliographical references.
ISBN P-941405-24-9 (pbk.)
1. Suffering—Religious aspects—Christianity.   2. Christian life—1960–
3. Spiritual healing.   I. Title.
BV4909.M375   1993
248.8'6—dc20   93-13946
                                                   CIP

Scripture taken from the HOLY BIBLE, NEW INTERNATIONAL
VERSION, Copyright© 1973, 1978, 1984 International Bible Society.

Printed in the United States of America
First Edition
10 9 8 7 6 5 4 3 2 1

To the memory of Rebecca Canady, my grandmother,
who told me about Jesus when I was a child. She
planted in me, years ago, the seeds of
ministry that are harvested today.

To my husband, Tony, who led me to receive Christ in
my most desperate hour and who continues to be my
hero. He has been my faithful companion, best friend,
and encourager. Hand in hand, we serve him.

To the memory of Rev. Ernie Rogers, my friend, whose
eyes saw in me what no one else's could. His love and
gentle encouragement challenged me to serve Jesus with
my testimony and gifts. I'll forever be grateful for the
many ways God used Ernie and his wife, Wanda,
as my spiritual parents.

A special thank you to Tracy Sayring for her support
in seeing this project completed.

Contents

Dear Reader,

During the years I cried out to God for help, I didn't have the benefit of professional counseling, a support group, or even a church that understood my fears and heartache. I had to become dependent on God for the answers because he was all I had. I learned that God, his Son, his Word, and prayer were the keys to unlock my emotional prison.

From Victim to Victor is a personal study guide that reaches into hurting hearts and lifts the pain to God for healing. I wrote it for Christians who need help letting go of the excess emotional baggage from guilt, rejection, abandonment, and loss caused by life's painful circumstances.

The purpose of this workbook is to offer love, encouragement, and ministry. How you got to where you are is not always as important as what you are doing with the pain now. What is going on in your heart ... in your relationships with family and friends ... in your relationship with Jesus Christ?

The recipes for healing, along with their challenging application, come from an accumulation of personal experience with God's healing power in my life. They reflect my seven years of teaching these biblical principles through counseling individuals, facilitating support groups, and speaking to groups.

The emotional healing process is much like a roller coaster ride—feelings of being on top and feelings of spiraling downward. As you begin to be in touch with your feelings, this up and down ride becomes frequent. One consolation is that, as on the roller coaster, at least you are moving forward. I pray that as you lean on Jesus to help you, he will reveal himself to you in a way you never knew possible. Only through Jesus and the power of the Holy Spirit can we be set free from the past's prison.

Many people find it helpful to go through a study like this with the support of others who understand how they feel. *From Victim to Victor* can be used in such a group or as an individual exercise.

Today doesn't have to be yesterday's prison. I hope that through this study, you, too, will know the joy and the victory of the Lord.

In his service,
Yvonne Martinez

Yesteryears

Sad, cruel memories of
life's short path
thunder in your mind.

The clouds engulf you
singing the pain
of yesterday's great fears.

But trust the Savior
by your side
to blow away the storm.

Pick up your banner
shout new praises
the victory has been won.

The foe has already
lost the war
through Calvary's crimson flow.

Don't let the tears
of yesteryears
wash the Son from your life today.

Don't let the tears
of yesteryears
wash away today.

—Yvonne Martinez

Beginning the Journey
from Victim to Victor

Many of us have trouble with trust. Risking being real is scary when we've masked, denied, or buried our needs. But, as you go through this study, take heart: You will benefit from it to the degree you emotionally invest in it.

Remember, you are working on *your* issues and problems. With that in mind, the only rule is that you don't focus on other people or their problems.

To get the most from this study, complete each reflective question and journaling exercise. I also recommend that during your daily devotional time you follow a routine that includes reading your Bible. Focus on Psalm 51:6–12 often.

> Surely you desire truth in the inner parts;
> you teach me wisdom in the inmost place.
> Cleanse me with hyssop, and I will be clean;
> wash me, and I will be whiter than snow.
> Let me hear joy and gladness;
> let the bones you have crushed rejoice.
> Hide your face from my sins

and blot out all my iniquity.
Create in me a pure heart, O God,
and renew a steadfast spirit within me.
Do not cast me from your presence
or take your Holy Spirit from me.
Restore to me the joy of your salvation
and grant me a willing spirit, to sustain me.

Begin a journal to express your feelings to God. Ask God to reveal the truth about you and your relationships. Share your secret fears, anger, and dreams as openly as possible. You can use a plain lined notebook or a cloth covered blank book, whichever is more comfortable for you. Try to pour out your heart in this intimate time with God. Write in your journal daily. There are journaling exercises throughout this book, which you can integrate into your journal if you choose.

If keeping a daily journal seems like an awesome task, try asking yourself the following questions to get started. A sample response follows each.

How do I feel today?
I feel so afraid and lonely ...

When was the first time I ever felt like this?
I used to feel this way when Mom and Dad were gone and I had no one to talk to ...

How do these feelings (which are usually attached to memories) still affect me and my relationships?
Sometimes I still get angry at my mom/dad when I call

and they don't have time to talk to me. I wonder if you, Lord, will always be there ...

When you are done writing, wait for the ministry of the Holy Spirit. Write down anything you feel coming from God. We can be counseled, comforted, or corrected with just a few precious words from the Lord. Maybe he will remind you of a Scripture or give you a personal confirmation of his love. His reply will always match up with Scripture. That is how you can be confident what you hear comes from the Lord.

When I look back through my journal, I am reminded God saw me through each problem and doubt I had. His words of faithfulness in the midst of my trial gave me encouragement.

Finally, continue in fellowship with believers in Jesus. Make friends and reach out to others. Pray for others, especially your enemies. You can and should call on family or friends to pray with and support you through this process. If you are in professional counseling, let your counselor/therapist know about your commitment to this study.

Prayer

God, I thank you for the privilege of coming into your presence through Jesus Christ. Your Word tells me you knew me from the foundation of the world—you saw my unformed substance, called me by name, and even knew the number of hairs on my head. I couldn't possibly begin to

know you as you know me. You are aware of my every need, every hurt, and every desire. I invite you to be my minister and counselor. Open my heart, and unlock the doors of fear. I ask you to fill my life with the presence and power of your Holy Spirit. I submit this study to you and ask you to use it to help me. Thank you for sending Jesus to be my Advocate, my Savior, my Provider, my Healer.
In Jesus' name, I pray ... (add your own thoughts).

_____

_____

_____

_____

_____

_____

_____

_____

_____

_____

_____

Amen.

He brought them out of darkness and the deepest gloom and broke away their chains.
—Psalm 107:14

Portrait of a Victim

As I listen to people in individual and group counseling, a common thread weaves through their tragic testimonials of physical abuse, sexual abuse, emotional neglect, rejection, and loss. They are all victims, stuck in a pattern of thinking, believing they have no choices. They all carry emotional scars from their past circumstances. These wounds never healed. Instead, the wounds became little cancers that ate away at their hope and abilities. Their backgrounds vary, but their helplessness to change doesn't. That is why they reach out; they want help.

I want to share my self-portrait with you for two reasons. First, I want to let you know that I really do know how you feel. Second, I want to give you encouragement and hope. What God has done in my life, he can do in yours.

My story includes much of the same trauma I hear from others, except one thing is different. My story has a happy ending. The past pain in my life no longer breathes down my neck and hangs on my heels. Yesterday is no longer today's prison. However, it wasn't always that way...

My parents played cards in the living room. But the room I was invited to play in was dark. I lay, with my panties down, between the sheets of a bed. The man playing house with me was a stranger, the son of our host. He was probably only about eighteen years old, but he was a man to me. I was four. I never saw him again. So the day, the man, and the sexual assault turned into a dream that remained buried until God revealed it some thirty years later. Though unremembered, the event was the first in a long line of victimizations.

My dad was an alcoholic and spent most of my earliest years in and out of prison. His parole brought unwelcome tension. My mom feared him, and so did I. He had a dominating and abrasive personality; he had broken Mom's nose and threatened her life. I loved my mom. But I didn't understand how she could love him. My last night with him was a nightmare.

He came in late, angry, and drunk. I was nine years old and supposed to be asleep, but I heard the fighting, then my mom's cries for help. As I opened their bedroom door, I saw my naked father tearing at my mother's pajamas. He saw me, covered himself, and pushed me from the room. The door slammed against my head and I felt dizzy. The next thing I remember was my mother taking my brother, sister, and me to Grandma's house. Grandma's had always been our hiding place.

In those days, divorce, a lengthy procedure, required evidence of wrong doing. I was asked to testify on my mother's behalf. But, fortunately, other evidence sufficed, and I didn't have to testify. Their divorce was granted.

My father, however, persisted in harassing us, and his presence was a constant threat. He peered into our windows in the middle of the night. I heard the bushes move and imagined an awful monster waiting to devour me.

He had visiting rights, but he didn't want to see me. I believed he knew I would have testified against him. Once, when I answered the telephone, he told me, "You turned against me, and I am disowning you. I don't ever want to see you again. You aren't my daughter anymore, and as far as I am concerned you don't exist."

I was afraid of him and didn't want to see him. Nevertheless, his words were like sharp knives that cut deep into my heart. I really didn't understand why he didn't like me, but I reasoned I must be a pretty awful little girl if my daddy did not want me. I covered the hurt with hate and told everyone I hated him. How else could I have reacted at the age of ten? My mother had been his victim, but so had I.

My adolescence sent me on a tremendous search for love. My mother remarried, and her drinking problems became evident. I spent most of my time alone, frequently going home from school "sick." Friends were unfaithful, and I yearned for meaningful relationships. My mother told me not to become serious about boys, but boys were my constant focus. I went looking for love in all the wrong places.

My grandma tried to tell me about Jesus. I prayed on Sunday, but by Monday I was sure even Jesus had forgotten about me.

I escaped into marriage at age eighteen, believing it would last forever. I married into a life of motorcycles, beer, and parties. The moments of passion and companionship were few. My husband lacked a good job and was irresponsible.

Two years into my marriage, I became pregnant. I thought finally I would have someone to love and someone to love me. My husband, on the other hand, saw the child as more responsibility.

Because I wanted to believe he cared, I accepted his excuses of having to work late, even all night long.

However, my husband's frequent absence and lack of concern eventually forced a confrontation. The truth hurt. He was seeing another woman, and he didn't know if he loved me. I tried to pull him back by controlling and manipulating him, but that didn't work. He had even been unfaithful the night I was in labor. He had violated my trust; I divorced him. As a single mom at twenty, I stuffed the feelings of betrayal and rejection down deep and began again.

Life went on, and I met Eric. We worked together and began dating. We fell in love. Well ... I fell in love first, as usual. I always did.

He had served in the Marines in Vietnam and now worked full time and attended college part time. I was impressed! After eighteen months, he asked me to marry him. My knight in shining armor had arrived. I couldn't believe my good fortune; he really loved me.

We had a small wedding and a weekend honeymoon. We settled into a little house nestled under a tree. He wanted me to quit work and stay home to be a wife and mother. Life had new meaning, and I thought surely this marriage would last forever. Then, just when everything was so perfect, it all came tumbling down.

I had kissed him good-bye about 9:30 that Saturday morning, and we had made plans to eat lunch together. At noon, a police car pulled into the driveway. Eric had been in an accident and was in critical condition. He was in intensive care.

Blood had run from his eyes and his ears. He was in a coma and had a brain stem injury. Nerve endings from the brain to his body were traumatized, and there was no way now of knowing how much mental damage he had sustained. The neurosurgeons told me if he survived he might have the mentality of a two-year-old, no memory at all, or—worse yet—he might just stay in the coma.

The doctors were not very encouraging, yet they did all they could. Even as I saw my world begin to crumble, I wouldn't give up hope. But hope just wasn't enough. Twenty-one days later, he died. The fighting and praying were over. I had dropped from 116 to 103 pounds. I had slept at the hospital for three weeks, stood by his bed, and watched his strong body fight to live. Now I laid my head on his chest and listened for life, but it was gone. We had only been married two months and thirteen days. And it was over. He died on September 3, my son's birthday.

Everywhere I turned, people patted me on the back and told me, "Don't cry, it will all be OK. You're young, you'll find someone else." I didn't want anyone else, and it wasn't OK. I was twenty-two years old with two marriages behind me. What could I possibly have to look forward to? What could be left after failing so many times? I thought I must be doing something terribly wrong and God must be punishing me. Guilt intensified the hurt. With nowhere to turn, I once again stuffed my feelings down and started life over. I wondered if I was grown up now. Holding my head up, I did what everyone expected me to do. I found someone new.

A few weeks into my new relationship, I found bruises and marks on my son's body. I confronted my boyfriend, and he denied everything. But no one else could have hurt Scott. After three trips to the doctor, I ended the relationship. The thought of my boyfriend hurting my son left me sick to my stomach.

I took what insurance money was left after Eric's funeral expenses and bought a business designing wigs and hairpieces. I've always had a creative flair and felt comfortable with this challenge. This way I would have control of my future. I negotiated the transaction, made the deposit, and in a few months I'd be all set. Inside though, I felt lonely and afraid. Bad dreams plagued me nightly. It seemed I could again hear the bushes rattle against my bedroom window, like they had so many years before. I hated being alone. I didn't feel safe in the dark.

To counter all the negative, I plunged into my business. This challenging and fun outlet gave me a nice break from the recent disasters. Customers often walked in the store and asked for the owner. I'd proudly say, "I'm the owner." To which they would answer I seemed too young. I'd explain that my husband had died, and I'd used insurance money to start the business. They'd remark I looked too young to be a widow. It seemed ironic to me to hear I was too young. I felt like an old woman. I guess I was too young for everything except pain. Life had been tough, but it would soon get tougher.

Time passed, and I was still single. The business was doing well, and I was in the market for a second store. I'd bought a house and had been dating someone fairly regularly. Everyone thought I had made it. What more could I want? On the outside everything was pretty cool, but inside there was a lonely, empty little girl. I wanted to be married, and my son needed a father. But I learned not to talk too much since no one had answers.

The steady relationship I was involved in wasn't the best, but that wasn't unusual. I always settled for second best. I didn't deserve the best, so why try, I reasoned. He was hard on my son and had hit me hard enough to send me to the doctor's office with blurry vision. He wouldn't marry me and he wouldn't let me go. I thought I loved him, and I thought he would change if we got married. I knew if I could be good enough, he wouldn't get mad at me. I pushed and pleaded until he finally said he'd marry me. It didn't take long for me to realize I had made another mistake. This marriage, I hoped, wouldn't last forever.

He continued to treat Scott with a heavy hand, and I didn't like it. If I intervened, he would only become more emotionally abusive. It seemed I didn't have a chance. He managed to bring out the worst in me—jealousy, insecurity, guilt, and fear. I stopped seeing most of my friends because he didn't like them. I had only been married a few months, and already I was trapped. I couldn't see it then, but I had become a battered wife and my son an abused stepchild.

I poured myself into the business, served on the shopping center's committee, and was elected president of our Merchant's Association. At least within the community and among my peers I had respect and recognition. I went ahead and bought a second store.

One busy Saturday I worked alone. At 5:00, closing time, I was waiting for a late customer, so I'd left the door unlocked while I swept the back room. The bell rang to let me know someone had come into the store. Thinking it was my late customer, I said, "I'll be right there." As I turned toward the front, I faced the barrel of a pistol and heard, "Turn around or I'll blow your head off."

I turned around and felt a revolver against the back of my head. "Do as I say, or I'll blow your _____ head off," he said. Never before had I been so terrified. I couldn't stop the urine from running down my legs. I believed I was going to die.

I had an urge to run, but I stood frozen. I knew I couldn't outrun a bullet. I concentrated on not fainting. I felt sure if I did, he would just get mad and kill me. He kept the gun pressed to my head and walked me through the store, demanding all the money. He even demanded the change from my purse. I handed over all my cash. Then he moved the gun to my back and ordered me to undress. I complied. He covered my head with a laundry bag, forced me onto the cement floor, and raped me. All the while he held the gun pressed against my temple.

Still threatening to shoot, he forced me into the bathroom and warned me not to tell anyone or call the police. He said if I did, he would return to kill me.

12

In a few minutes, I heard the store bell again. I waited a little longer before coming out of the bathroom. Seeing he was gone, I called the police. I spoke almost without thinking, "Help me, I think I was raped." As I did, I glanced at the clock. It was only 5:30—the longest half hour of my life. I was thankful to be alive.

Patrol cars, an ambulance, and paramedics came roaring up in front of the store. I protested about going to the hospital, but everyone insisted. The policeman defined *rape* and I was convinced I had, indeed, been raped. The words *embarrassment* and *humiliation* simply do not express the shame I felt.

The hospital staff did its job clinically, without any expression of sympathy. The police took reports, photos, and evidence. The hardest part, facing my family, was yet to come.

I knew that my husband wouldn't believe I had been raped. He would probably think I had enticed or somehow invited this man's behavior. I felt more afraid of my husband's reaction than of the rapist's return. All I wanted to do was go home and shower the ugliness from my body. I tried, but showers didn't help.

I spent the next day with the police working on composite pictures and looking at photographs. It helped to know I had their support, but still I felt helpless and vulnerable.

The rapist was caught, then escaped. The police monitored my activities because of his threats against my life. The intensity of the crime was compounded by newspaper publicity. Customers, business associates, and friends knew. I felt marked, ashamed, and guilty.

My marriage relationship grew more stressful because of the rape, and I felt almost crazy seeking comfort in the arms of another abuser, my husband. My emotional composure slipped. My defenses and ability to protect myself disappeared. My strength began to fade, as did my hope. For the first time, I felt emotionally paralyzed.

The next three months passed quickly. Then my father died. I had only seen him once since that awful conversation when I was nine and he disowned me. I wasn't sure why, but I had to go to his funeral. After all, he was my dad, and I should be there.

The plane landed in hot, humid Florida. Relatives I hadn't seen in years greeted me. But they weren't too happy to see me; they assumed I had come to pick over the estate for my share.

My father died from alcoholism at age fifty-two. He'd spent the years I knew nothing about in and out of prison. He had remarried and divorced. I visited the small, old house he lived in. It was dirty and had cockroaches.

His few possessions included several pictures he had painted in prison. I realized uncomfortably where my artistic flair had come from. His paintings reminded me of mine. My father was a big part of my life whether I wanted to admit it or not.

I felt nervous in the simple funeral home. The open casket revealed that my father was still handsome. Something strange triggered in my heart when I looked at his face. I began to cry from deep within. "Oh Daddy, please tell me you love me," I cried. "Daddy, where were you when all the bad guys tried to hurt me? Please, Daddy, just tell me you care." I cried for the daddy I never had. I wanted him to hold me and tell me he loved me. I wanted him to tell me he would protect me.

At that moment I realized why I had come to Florida. I was still waiting for my dad to tell me he loved me. I thought all my pain could have been comforted and my stress relieved if only I knew he cared. But I would never know. He would never tell me. I cried for a lost relationship, for the years I could never recover, for the dad I never had.

No one understood my emotion. People asked why, if I cared, I hadn't tried to see him when he was alive. How could anyone ever know the torment he had caused all those years?

At the funeral, someone pressed a blond cedar box into my hands. I opened it and found a beautiful white Bible inside. As I look back, I see the Lord comforting me even then. He said, "Little child, I will be your Father. I will be your Comforter. I will be your Protector. I love you even when it seems no one else does." I couldn't hear God then and left Florida feeling emptier than ever, except for that little cedar box I tucked ever so gently into my luggage.

The time away had given me opportunity to think about my life—where I had been and where I was going.

What little tenderness I received from my husband after the rape disappeared. His teasing and ridicule became more intimidating than ever. He liked to make me feel small and worthless so he could feel big and important. One night he turned out the lights, then he threw firecrackers into my shower and laughed at my screams. If I tried to fight, I would only lose. I knew I couldn't last too much longer.

The rape had done something to my mind. I knew I would never be the same again. I daydreamed about Eric and how much I had loved him. Or was it that I dreamed of his loving me? These thoughts only brought the reality of his death in focus. I had no hope. I needed someone or something to help me.

Arriving home meant facing my life. My marriage had become a war of emotional games. The rape had been far more than physical: It had been a rape of my ability to defend myself, a rape of my soul. My father's death finalized my unworthiness. I could not have a relationship with a man. I gave in; fear and guilt had won. I took pills to sleep and pills to stay awake. I even drank alcohol, which I detested.

The police caught the rapist again and set another trial date. The man wanted to waive his right to an attorney and defend himself. The court granted his request, which gave him access to all the evidence against him. The reports included personal information about me: my home address and telephone number, the location of my second store.

I began to receive phoned threats from an intimidating voice, both at my business and at home. I was the one who could put him back in prison. The threatening words he spoke after he raped me rang loudly in my ears, "If you tell, I'll kill you." My overwhelming fear of leaving the house or being alone mounted, and my world became smaller and smaller. I sold the business where the rape had taken place and tried to have someone with me at all times.

The stress and tension also caused physical problems. It had been years since I had a doctor's check-up. A pap smear disclosed cancer, and I was told I had five years to live. The word *cancer* was shocking and ugly, almost as ugly as rape. Surgery was the next step. I had a hysterectomy. I was 26. Life had been unfair.

The trial came and the rapist received far less punishment than he deserved. The courts call it plea-bargaining. I lost my excitement for my business and my energy for living. My husband emotionally abused me with threats such as, "If you ever try to leave me, I will cut you up in little pieces and bury you in the field across the street." He called this teasing.

At night, beads of sweat formed on my brow and my perspiration wet the sheets as fear gripped me. I could lay motionless for hours, barely breathing. Sleep came only after I was exhausted from wrestling with tormenting thoughts. I hadn't been able to stop the merry-go-round of events that held me captive. I believed I would die by the age of thirty. Thoughts of suicide dashed through my mind.

As I searched for comfort from the long terror-filled nights, often a childhood song, "Jesus loves me this I know..." would flush away my fear. I wondered if Jesus could love me. "If you are there," I prayed, "please help me. Oh, God, please help me." Little did I know that Jesus was listening to my plea.

My fear of staying with my husband became stronger than my fear of leaving, so I planned an escape. My son and I divorced the abusive marriage, left the house I owned, and tried to start again.

Yes, you're right. I met another man. But Tony was a Christian. He led me to receive Jesus as my personal savior.

17

I found new hope through Jesus Christ. Having the assurance of heaven gave me a challenge to survive as my fear of death diminished. And, of course, death wasn't in God's immediate plans for me. My next doctor's check-up revealed the surgery successfully removed all the cancer. No further treatments were necessary. I knew Jesus was planning my life.

Eighteen months later Tony and I married. We grew strong together, and I blossomed with the freshness of a new romance and the love of God. However, mixed with my joy were deep-seated problems from my past, which surfaced frequently. My inability to confront them caused strain and frustration. I wanted this relationship to work, but I made Tony the brunt of my anger, bitterness, and insecurity. He was patient, though, and didn't try to fix me or my problems.

He understood it wasn't him or his fault, it was me. I was a woman full of guilt, fear, rejection, and condemnation. My wounds were concealed behind a mask of confidence and self-reliance. Sores not visible to the naked eye surfaced only when I couldn't hold back my anger and tears. The problem was the accumulation of so many tragedies that were too big for any spiritual Band-Aid to cover. I was stuck in an emotional prison. Even as a Christian, I was still a victim.

Portrait of a Victor

God began to slowly remove the Band-Aid and shed his love into my wounded life, not only to stop the infection but to heal me. Healing came over the next three years—not all at once and not in a neat step-by-step fashion. Sometimes it seemed that for every two steps forward I took one step backward.

My biggest breakthroughs came when I knelt with my prayer journal, lamenting to God, listening to his presence, feeling his love and forgiveness, and trying to practice them in my life. In addition to journaling, I called upon my husband and friends to pray for me when I felt out of control. I read books on emotional healing and tried to learn as much as I could about the effects of abuse. I knew God was working in my life, but I couldn't see the end result. Then one day I realized that I was experiencing more days of joy and fewer days of torment. Finally, after five years as a Christian, I was coming out of a long, dark tunnel into the brightness of a new day.

Today is even brighter. For the lost relationship with my dad, I now have a heavenly father who promises never to abandon me. In place of the failed marriages, God gave me a wonderful husband. This year we celebrate fourteen years of marriage. During those years we adopted three more children and Scott married a precious girl, Alicia, whom I dearly love. My mother found help for her drinking and has been a Christian for over ten years. I'm so glad God is alive and well and still in the reconciliation business!

About eight years ago, when I felt a tug to reach out to others, I asked God to reveal to me what he had done and how he had changed me. I got out my journal and began to write about the phases I had grown through and the transitions I had experienced. Each phase was pivotal, but it took all of them combined to bring me into the fullness of Christ and make me feel complete. They continue to help me grow close to Christ.

Much like a baker's recipe, you can't taste the quality of the finished product until all the ingredients are measured, mixed, and baked. As the Lord gave me the ingredients, I tested them and refined them. Gradually, with the help of a loving church, good friends, and prayer, I found the winning combination. The recipe for healing that changed my life forever included the following six key "ingredients":

1. I learned who Jesus really is and who I am in him.
2. I learned to face the secrets of my past and flush out repressed feelings.
3. I learned to face my own sin and the way I hurt others because of my pain.
4. I learned how to surrender both my past and my guilt by trusting in God.
5. I learned what forgiveness is, how to forgive others and myself, and how to receive forgiveness.
6. I learned I was in a spiritual battle and that I had the tools, through Jesus, to recognize the enemy, fight, and win.

Working through this book, which is organized around these healing ingredients, will bring you hope and victory. Once we put our past to rest, we continue in the life-long process of sanctification, that is, being conformed into the image of Christ. With our past reconciled, we are free to celebrate today.

Reflections

Just as I have written out my portrait, I would like you to do the same. Through this exercise, honestly evaluate where you are and what circumstances have led you to this point. Change begins when we discover how we are stuck in patterns of thinking and living. Don't rush through this exercise; take your time and think through the details of your life. Be as *honest* and *specific* as possible.

_____

_____

_____

_____

_____

_____

_____

_____

_____

_____

_____

_____

_____

_____

_____

_____

_____

_____

_____

_____

_____

_____

_____

_____

_____

_____

_____

_____

After writing out my portrait, or testimony, and rereading it I can see where most of my fears and problems began. I can define specific hurts and losses as well as my reactions to them. This exercise helped me discern where I needed God's healing.

Reread your story and answer the following questions:

Describe any incidents you wrote about that resulted from emotional, verbal, physical, or sexual abuse.

_____

_____

_____

_____

What left-over feelings do you have from these events?

_____

_____

_____

_____

In what way have you covered or buried your hurt because the pain was too great to bear?

_____

_____

_____

In what way were you rejected or betrayed?

_____

_____

_____

_____

Knowing in your heart the person(s) who hurt you, have you been able to forgive them? If yes, describe the process. If no, what would it take?

_____

_____

_____

_____

How have your present relationships been infected by your past hurts?

_____

_____

_____

In what ways do you feel emotionally paralyzed?

_____

_____

_____

I hope this exercise has given you a clearer under-standing of the issues in your life that need God's healing. The remaining chapters will help you apply the healing ingredients to your hurts.

As you work through these principles, I want to assure you that though the process may be difficult, like the roller coaster I described earlier, the rewards will be worth the difficulty.

Prayer

Lord, it is painful to rehearse my life, much of it is filled with doubts and fears. I ask for your courage to stay focused and for the courage not to run from the hurt. Enable me, through your Holy Spirit, to trust you with this process.
In Jesus' name, I pray … (add your own thoughts).

_____

_____

_____

_____

Amen.

"But for you who revere my name, the sun of righteousness will rise with healing in its wings. And you will go out and leap like calves released from the stall. Then you will trample down the wicked; they will be ashes under the soles of your feet…"
—Malachi 4:2–3

Learning Who Jesus Is and Who We Are in Him

Relationship with God

As Christians, all of our hope, help, and healing rests in Jesus' death and resurrection. Each day we awake to the fullness of what that represents as its privileges and responsibilities become active in our hearts and lives.

Yet, I remember in the beginning how my relationship with Jesus was unclear. It was a relationship plagued with misunderstanding, guilt, and fear. I felt isolated even within a church family.

Today, a great deal of my counseling time is spent correcting wrong concepts and beliefs about God. I have learned through my own experience and from others that what we believe about God directly affects our healing in the areas of rejection and low self-esteem.

I know some things about the president of the United States. I know where he resides, what his duties are, and when he is on an overseas tour. But if I were asked about his personal thoughts or how to telephone him in an emergency I couldn't reply. Even if I read his autobiography,

27

although I would have more information about him, we would still be strangers.

The same is true with God. Simply knowing about him isn't enough. He wants us to know him, not just know about him. God doesn't want us to be strangers. Nor does he want us to have false beliefs about him, no matter what authority figure gave them to us. In fact, he desires intimate communion. Not only has he given us an extensive autobiography, he has included the instructions for personal fellowship through Jesus Christ.

To assume we know God's will and desire for us without really knowing him or his nature leaves us relying on our own faulty judgment. Let's look at a few examples of wrong assumptions about God and our circumstances.

Cindy loved God and was active in her church until about a year ago, when her young son was killed in an automobile accident. Deep down inside she believed God may have taken her son away as punishment for an abortion she had as a teenager.

Dale had been a Christian for many years, but on occasion he purchased pornographic literature from a local adult bookstore. He asked God to heal him of his sexual struggle. After losing numerous battles with temptation, Dale believed even God couldn't help him.

A young Christian man was suspected of committing a morally degrading crime and was held in a local jail. He knew his innocence, but the accusation and humiliation were more than he could bear. After a few hours, the initial investigation proved his innocence. But when his captors went to release him, they found he had hung himself with his belt.

Israel made a similar mistake in believing the Lord had led them into despair. They asked, "Why is the Lord bringing us to this land only to let us fall by the sword?" (Num. 14:3). Over and over they thought that bad circumstances amounted to a fatal situation. The result was idolatry and the death of many.

From these illustrations in wrong thinking about God, we can learn three valuable principles.

1. As long as we can trust the Lord and wait on him, we have an opportunity to see his ability to rescue us.
2. Losing the ability to make choices removes hope.
3. Choosing a desperate course of action often results in disastrous consequences.

Most mistrust results from the mistake of believing God is like some person we know—someone who failed to love, nourish, or accept; or someone who failed to love enough to correct and set limits.

Reflections

Describe a situation where you were impatient for God to rescue you.

_____

_____

What courses of action did you take to try to solve the problem on your own?

What was the result?

Before continuing, ask God to give you understanding and insight to his Word through the following prayer:

Lord, as I come before you, I ask you to reveal yourself to me in a new way. Through your Word, correct my wrong thinking about you. I want to receive everything you want

*for me and the fullness of all that you want me to be. Help
my unbelief. Allow me to see myself through your eyes.
In Jesus' name I pray ...* (add your own thoughts).

_____

_____

_____

_____

_____

Amen.

The only way to have an accurate picture of God is to
go to his Word. In the following exercise, look up the
characteristics of God to gain a clear understanding of who
he is.

Names of God

*Look up the following biblical references and list the names
that reflect his authority and power.*

- Genesis 17:1   Almighty God _____
- Matthew 6:26 _____
- Exodus 3:14   _____

*Look up the following biblical references and list the various
aspects of God's nature.*

- Genesis 22:14   The Lord will provide
- Exodus 17:15   _____
- Judges 6:24   _____
- Ezekiel 48:35   _____
- Jeremiah 23:6   _____
- Jeremiah 33:16 _____

What do the following Bible promises tell us about God?

- Isaiah 43:1–3   God is with me
- John 14:18   _____
- Psalm 102:17   _____
- Proverbs 18:10 _____

Names of Jesus

Look up the following references and list a few of the names attributed to Jesus.

- Hebrews 5:9   Source of Eternal Salvation
- Isaiah 9:6   _____
- Romans 11:26   _____
- Revelation 1:5   _____
- John 1:29   _____
- Acts 10:36   _____

Often in the search for answers to personal problems, we overlook the basics of our faith and go looking for a new solution. The sad result of this is seen when Christians begin believing the short-lived promises of false religions.

God has already provided everything we will ever need in his Son, Jesus. Look up these Scriptures that reinforce what Jesus has done for us through salvation, justification, and sanctification.

How are we saved?

- 1 John 4:14 _____
- Acts 4:12 _____
- Romans 10:9, 10 _____
- 1 Timothy 4:9, 10 _____

How are we justified?

- Romans 5:1 _____
- Galatians 3:24 _____

How are we sanctified?

- John 17:17 _____
- 1 Corinthians 1:30 _____
- Ephesians 5:26 _____
- 2 Timothy 2:21 _____

*Read the first chapter of Ephesians. This chapter is full
of God's blessings to us who believe and a reminder of what
a heritage we have in Jesus. What does it tell you?*

_____

_____

_____

_____

_____

Jesus' words from John 8:31, 32 should spur us on to
learn about and accept God's truth "… 'If you hold to my
teaching … you will know the truth, and the truth will set
you free.'"

Prayer

*Lord, thank you for showing me the truth of your Word. Help
me to hang on to your truth as you reveal yourself to me. I
want my mind transformed that I may know you more fully.
Thank you for your faithfulness to me.
In Jesus' name, I pray …* (add your own thoughts).

_____

_____

_____

_____

Amen.

Journaling Exercise One

Write down your doubts or fears about God in the table provided. Take your time and be honest. Allow all thoughts to be experienced. There may be times when you say to yourself:

> "I know what the Bible says, but I just can't get it into my heart."
> "I don't want to hear a bunch of Scriptures."
> "I don't understand what this has to do with my problem."
> "I read the Word and pray every day, but nothing changes."
> "I can't feel God."

Or, you may feel God is like an abuser who ordered disaster into your life or a neglector who happened to be out to lunch when disaster hit. After exploring your feelings, find a Scripture verse that gives you encouragement or reassurance, and write it down opposite your feeling statement.

Write Your Doubts and Fears about God	*Find a Scripture Verse that Encourages and Reassures*
Example: I feel like God never hears my prayers	The eyes of the Lord are righteous and his ears are attentive to their cry. Psalm 34:15

God can never forgive my adultry.	As far as the east is from the west, so far has he removed our transgressions from us. Psalm 103:12

❖ ❖ ❖

_____	_____
_____	_____
_____	_____
_____	_____
_____	_____

❖ ❖ ❖

_____	_____
_____	_____
_____	_____
_____	_____
_____	_____

❖　❖　❖

_____　　_____

_____　　_____

_____　　_____

_____　　_____

_____　　_____

Journaling Exercise Two

Now write about your self-doubt and fears. Remember that God is not surprised by anything you feel or think. You aren't telling God anything he doesn't already know. Your wrong interpretation of God is a key to why you are stuck in your circumstances. Then, as before, find a Scripture verse that offers you hope. Write it down opposite your feeling statement.

Write About Your Self-Doubt and Fears	*Find a Scripture Verse that Offers Hope*
Example: I feel alone	"I will never leave you; never will I forsake you." Hebrews 13:5

❖　❖　❖

I am too weak to fight temptation.	God is our refuge and strength an ever-present help in trouble. Psalm 46:1

37

_____   _____

_____   _____

_____   _____

_____   _____

_____   _____

❖   ❖   ❖

_____   _____

_____   _____

_____   _____

_____   _____

_____   _____

❖   ❖   ❖

_____   _____

_____   _____

_____   _____

_____   _____

❖   ❖   ❖

_____   _____

_____   _____

_____   _____

_____   _____

_____   _____

Prayer

Pray and confess to God inaccurate thoughts or beliefs that you discovered as you journaled. Also, ask him to show you beliefs that you may not even be aware of, but that have wrongly influenced the way you understand God. A suggested prayer format follows:

First, admit wrong attitudes or beliefs.

God, according to your Word, I confess that what I thought about you was inaccurate because ... (continue in your own words).

_____

_____

_____

_____

Then, ask God for forgiveness.

Please forgive me for not believing your Word and for believing a lie ... (continue in your own words).

_____

_____

_____

_____

Finally, acknowledge God's grace and forgiveness.

Thank you for being faithful and for teaching me what is right. I choose to accept what your Word says. Help me apply it to my life in these areas ... (continue in your own words).

_____

_____

_____

_____

_____

_____

Amen.

"...my people are destroyed from lack of knowledge."
—Hosea 4:6

Facing My Secrets

Self-Examination

Once we begin studying it, we see God's Word was never meant to be a Band-Aid but a mirror that reflects to us our thoughts and attitudes. When we are confronted with the truth about God, we are also confronted with the truth about ourselves.

Talking and writing about feelings and things that have happened to us is an important step in facing and sorting out the truth.

As a new Christian, I lived in fear about my past. When I could no longer hide from my feelings, I began writing and then talking about them. It was my next step to freedom.

As you begin this lesson, pray with me:

Lord, you know my heart, and nothing has ever been hidden from you. You created me and know everything that has ever happened to me. Encourage me to tell you the truth about what I am about to face. I desire your healing and freedom. I no longer want to be stuck in an emotional prison. Educate me through your wisdom. Bring understanding to my mind.

Help me share my feelings and events and thank you for being a good listener. I invite you to be my counselor and minister. In Jesus' name I pray.
Amen.

Look up Psalm 139:13–16. How does this describe the wonder of your uniqueness and the special care God gave your identity?

_____

_____

_____

_____

One of God's gifts to us is the ability to laugh and feel joy as well as to cry and feel sadness. Our feelings are meant to work for us as an indicator of how we're doing. When our gauge begins signaling "alert ... hurt feelings ... painful memory ... shame," we sometimes put a pillow over the alarm. Problems become intensified when we detach our feelings from events. This is called denial.

In the Psalms, David continually cries out and expresses his feelings to God. God wants us to express our feelings, too. In the story of the Samaritan woman in the Gospel of John (John 4:1–26), Jesus pointed out she had been married five times and was now living with another man. Rather than allow her to bury her past and its pain, Jesus brought it to her attention.

If you know you're dealing with one specific issue like divorce, abortion, or rape, then you already have an awareness of your problem. However, even when we understand what has happened, sometimes we don't know how to get beyond it.

Sometimes a surface problem can, like a curtain, hide a deeper, more significant issue. This happened, for example, to a woman attending a divorce recovery group. While discussing her feelings about her unfaithful husband and failing marriage, she realized an even deeper struggle with rejection and betrayal from a childhood trauma involving her alcoholic father.

When we avoid coping with life's hurts by burying the pain, guilt and shame become our emotional hangovers.

By finally looking at my past I learned to separate my guilty feelings into two categories. Both categories rest under the umbrella of sin. First, I caused grief to other people and especially to God. True guilt is a consequence of disobeying God's laws. And it can be acknowledged, repented from, and forgiven. I will discuss this in depth in the next chapter.

Second, others caused me grief through their actions and words. I had wrongly assumed responsibility and guilt for them. No matter how hard I tried, I couldn't repent from them. They weren't my sins. False guilt is relieved when we refuse to carry the responsibility for something God doesn't hold us accountable for.

Ask the Lord to show you how you contributed to a situation. You may discover that you didn't. Once the question of responsibility is answered, guilt can be dealt with.

This seems like a simple thing to do, of course. But many people just aren't sure how to separate the true from

43

the false. Somewhere along the line, they believed—either through assumption or accusation—they were responsible for a situation that brought a negative consequence.

Mary was molested by her brother. She told a friend who promptly said, "Well, my brother tried that stuff and I told him, 'No!'" Mary felt guilt because she hadn't told her brother no; she believed she had allowed the molestation.

Bob frequently yelled and sometimes even hit his wife when she failed to keep the house spotless. His wife, Meg, believed that if she could only do things better, he would stop. She said she wasn't a good wife.

Susan rode her bike down an unsafe road from school, even though her parents had asked her to take a safer, alternate route. With anguish in her voice, she told me it was her fault she was attacked and raped by two older boys because she did not follow her parents' instructions.

At a very emotionally vulnerable time, while I was dealing with the very issues of this chapter, I told a pastor that I had been raped. He tipped his glasses, nodded his head, and said, "Oh." A few Sundays later his sermon included a briefing about how women "ask" to be raped. His view of rape was obviously distorted.

To correctly answer the question of responsibility in these and our own situations, we need to have an understanding of abuse and its effects.

Abuse has many faces including emotional, physical, sexual, and ritualistic. It can be defined as wrongful, unreasonable, or harmful treatment by word or deed.

Emotional Abuse

Words are powerful. The writer of Proverbs 15:4 says, "The tongue that brings healing is a tree of life, but a deceitful tongue crushes the spirit."

Emotional abuse demeans a person's character and dignity and assaults self-esteem. "Sticks and stones may break my bones, but names will never hurt me" just isn't true.

A child's world can be built by words of encouragement and acceptance or destroyed by cruel, demeaning words. Neglect—the absence of words, time, or touch—leaves a child emotionally hungry, literally starved for attention.

With tears in his eyes, Robert told me his father had never hugged him or said, "I love you." Unfortunately, many children like Robert grow up never knowing if they are wanted or loved simply because they aren't told.

Types of emotional abuse include name calling, chronic criticism, unrealistic expectations, absence of affection, not listening, belittling, blaming, and public embarrassment.

Physical Abuse

Physical abuse results in bruises, black eyes, and broken bones; sometimes even death. Every blow causes damage to a person's dignity.

I can still recall the first time I was hit in the face. The degradation and humiliation greatly outweighed the physical pain.

Punishing (inflicting harm through anger), rather than disciplining (training to bring about correction), is abusive treatment. The child is left confused, unable to understand the parent's action.

Physical abuse can range from withholding meals or other necessities of life to violent and unpredictable outbursts.

Sexual Abuse

Child sexual abuse is the interaction (viewing or touching) between a child and adult, used for sexual stimulation of the adult.

Children who have been sexually abused are damaged emotionally and often report feelings of worthlessness, betrayal, and helplessness. Sexually abused people tend to make poor choices regarding relationships and have trouble with intimacy, especially in marriage.

Types of child sexual abuse can also include exposing a child to adults engaging in sexual activity, lusting after a child (who knows about it), telling sexually explicit jokes to a child, ridiculing parts of a child's body, and misinforming a child about sexual function. Sexual abuse among adults consists of any sexual activity against a person's will.

Ritualistic Abuse

Ritualistic abuse is usually connected to the ceremonial rites of cultists or satanists. Its damage is far reaching and often results in the need for specialized and trained counselors.

Unfortunately, Christian homes are not immune to the influence of abuse. About 50 percent of my clients grew up abused or neglected in Christian homes. The offenders sometimes held important roles in the church.

One middle-aged man had been raised by his uncle, who also happened to be his Sunday School teacher. The uncle would take him to church on Sunday, teach him about Jesus, then sexually abuse him during the week. The greatest obstacle this man had to overcome was the distorted image of Jesus that his uncle represented. He knew this intellectually, but every time he thought of Jesus, he saw his uncle's face.

Questions and confusion about God are sometimes difficult to resolve when trust has been violated by an adult, such as a parent, uncle, teacher, or pastor, who most represent Christ.

Many of us have had false assumptions about abuse. A few of them include:

Abuse Should Be Minimized

"I guess I should be grateful it wasn't worse. This has happened to lots of people." I hear that a lot in my counseling. In reality, abuse damages a person irrespective of duration, who the offender was, or the level of interaction. I like what Larry Crabb, a well-known author, said during one of his seminars: The size of the gun doesn't determine if you have been shot.

Abuse Heals with Time

"It has been five years now ... I shouldn't have to go and dig that stuff up now. I don't want to discuss it," people will say. However, time is not a healer—only a distancer from the pain.

Abuse Can Be Defined by the Act

"He never actually touched me, but I hated the way he looked at my body. I feel so stupid because I can't describe what he did." Remember, a person is abused when his or her dignity is diminished. It is unfair to the victim to imply a label be given to the event before feelings can be validated. I once heard someone say, "secrets are sickness and openness is wholeness." How true this statement is.

Sharing stories is a necessary and sometimes emotional event. Often people don't realize how they have avoided feelings until they talk or write about them. As you contemplate this, you may be wondering about confrontation. To ease your mind, confrontation isn't a prerequisite for healing. My father died before I ever became a Christian and began to deal with my pain. Therefore, I couldn't confront him directly. However, I could confront the truth through journaling about my feelings, and through prayer I found resolve.

If confrontation seems necessary, it should be done from a place of strength. Unless the offender recognizes and accepts his or her responsibility, you will set yourself up for more rejection and hurt.

If you are still in danger of being abused, you should temporarily refrain from that relationship until you and the offender can get some help.

Reflections

Go back and reread the overview of your life you wrote on page 21. Now choose a primary event in which you were hurt and write about it. For example, write in detail about what happened, who was involved, and what they said or did. Be specific and write as much as you need to.

Sometimes because of emotional strain, nervousness, or memory loss, events may seem mixed up. Don't be afraid to pause and regroup your thoughts. It is important to fully examine the event. Allow yourself to express your true feelings.

_____

_____

_____

_____

_____

_____

_____

_____

_____

_____

_____

_____

_____

_____

_____

_____

_____

_____

_____

_____

To help you evaluate your feelings concerning the event, complete the following journaling exercise.

Journaling Exercise Three

How has God showed you there are circumstances you are not responsible for?

_____

_____

_____

_____

Who was responsible? Why were they responsible?

_____

_____

_____

_____

_____

Describe your feelings about who was responsible.

_____

_____

_____

_____

How have you minimized or discounted these feelings?

_____

_____

_____

Repeat these exercises for other hurtful events you remember.

Write each responsible person a not-to-be-mailed letter. Remember that a not-to-be-mailed letter is *not to be mailed!* It doesn't have to be punctuated, proper, or perfect. This is an exercise in expression and isn't meant to be judged or corrected.

Follow this format for your letter, duplicating it for as many letters as you feel you need to write.

Dear _____,

You hurt me when you _____

_____

_____

_____

Because of what you did, I am still struggling with _____

_____

_____

52

_____

_____

At this time in my life, this is how I feel about you:

_____

_____

_____

Signed and dated _____

Read your letters out loud or to a friend who is supporting you through this process. Afterward it is sometimes helpful to destroy the letter(s) so they don't fall into the wrong hands.

Prayer

After completing your letter-writing exercise, pray for each person who hurt you.

Lord, I acknowledge my pain and loss and bring it before you. How grieved you must have been when you saw what happened and how devastating sin can be. I am reminded of your faithfulness. You'll never leave or forsake me, even when others will.

Today, I place false guilt where it belongs—in the hands of _____, the responsible person. Help me forgive him (her) and pray for his (her) healing.

Thank you for reminding me you were touched by affliction when you paid for the sins of the world. I also ask you to begin showing me how I have hurt others. I praise and thank you for the healing you are bringing in my life.

Before closing, wait and listen for anything you feel God may be saying to you. Learning to listen to God will be a great comfort. You can be assured what you feel or hear is from God when it lines up with what the Bible says. His impressions, songs, psalms, and words can bring true peace. This peace isn't an absence of conflict but the inner assurance that God cares for you. Write down anything you hear from God right now.

_____

_____

_____

_____

_____

Amen.

The dead man came out, his hands and feet wrapped with strips of linen, and a cloth around his face. Jesus said to them, "Take off the grave clothes and let him go."
—John 11:44

Facing My Sins

Self-Examination

Relinquishing false guilt is just one part of the twofold process of self-examination. Next is the often uncomfortable work in which the Holy Spirit reveals the sinful ways we have responded to what others have done. It is God's answer to our prayer from Psalm 51:6–12 to "create in me a pure heart."

I contributed to my victimization by not looking at how I hurt others because of my pain. Not only did I not look at it, I excused and justified it. I had to take responsibility for my sinful actions if I was to be emotionally free.

As children, we often needed self-protection to survive deprivation, neglect, or violence. As adults, our learned ways of protection can become the walls that close us in and keep everyone else, including God, out. They become the obstacles that block intimate relationships. In short, they are the roots of our sinful attitudes and actions.

A situation that occurred with my adopted daughter may help illustrate this. My daughter was bright, cheerful, and into everything, all the time! But when the babysitter commented on how good she was about bedtime, I was surprised. Bedtime usually meant endless pleading to stay up longer because she hated being alone in her room.

As a newborn my daughter had been abandoned. Then, as an infant, she'd had an illness that required twenty-four-hour care. Not being able to afford a nurse meant either my husband or I was with her at all times. After her adoption was final and she had outgrown the medical problems, we were able to occasionally leave her with a reliable babysitter. It seemed the only way she could cope with our absence was to hide in her bed, cover herself up, and go to sleep. Today, at seven years old, she still displays fear of being abandoned and is very uncooperative and sometimes rude toward others.

Children learn methods to protect themselves when they feel insecure or threatened. My daughter wasn't sinning when she attempted to protect herself as a child. She was coping with a situation that wasn't within her power to change. But as she grows older, I have to work and pray with her so her attitude toward others becomes pleasing to God.

Self-protective habits, especially those that are established in childhood, can become the broken glasses through which adults view their world. Adults living a child's learned patterns of coping become imprisoned, and the adult heart flutters and fights against the bars for freedom.

Adults who live their lives through a coping mechanism or from a defensive position don't believe or realize they have choices. They choose, by default, the same unfulfilling patterns. This helplessness or inability to choose something else fuels the lies that keep them trapped, and protective walls are reinforced with self-pity and anger.

They make decisions out of reactions rather than responsible actions. As a result, they expect or assume God, or someone else, will change them without their taking ownership of their actions or taking steps to change.

Feelings like revenge, hatred, anger, unforgiveness, and ambivalence are natural responses to being hurt. But when we harbor and protect them, we often reshape them into weapons to hurt ourselves or someone else. The coping mechanism or self-protective attitude reveals itself through sinful attitudes and actions.

Reacting out of our pain causes us to sin against others and God. By justifying our sin, we excuse or deny the thoughts or behaviors that hurt others. We may say, "This is just how I am," or "I've always been like this, and that is just how it is." By justifying our sin, we entertain the invitation to rebel against God and his Word. Finally, we discount true guilt, God's conviction for our sin, and deny Jesus' atoning work on the cross.

When God begins the work of showing us our sins, he brings to the surface not only those things we recognize, but also the attitudes we were completely unaware we carried. The Holy Spirit, called the Comforter or Counselor, brings the inward cleansing and the changing necessary "to be conformed to the likeness of his Son" (Rom. 8:29). Sanctification is required if we are to grow and mature as Christian ambassadors.

Nancy was in my group for help regarding childhood incest and abuse, and an adolescent sexual assault. Even though her deepest desire is to be a good mom, Nancy has difficulty handling her anger toward her child. Out of frustration, she resorts to the same abusive methods of punishment that were used on her as a child. Her son, in turn, hits and screams at children on the playground at school.

Nancy is seeing firsthand the consequences of her unresolved anger. The family patterns are hard to break, but with God's help, she is learning to separate her actions from those of her parents. By taking responsibility for her actions and choosing more effective methods of discipline, she *can* stop the abusive cycle.

Melissa was abandoned as a child and raised in a poor environment, but she vowed some day she would be somebody. Believing her body was a ticket to success, she became an escort. After two years, Melissa was arrested and convicted of prostitution. In jail she accepted Jesus, but after being released, she continued to be sexually active and subsequently had two abortions.

Melissa is depressed over the course of her life. She blames the abortions on her boyfriend, who insisted she terminate the pregnancies. Melissa's counselor is encouraging her to face her mistakes and take responsibility for her actions through giving and receiving forgiveness.

Jennifer's alcoholic parents abused her. Before she reached sixteen, in an attempt to find acceptance and attention, she left school and ran away from home. Her endless search for love led her to boys, gangs, and drugs. Then she became pregnant.

Jennifer didn't have a choice about her childhood abuse, but her response to her situation only complicated matters more. A Christian family took her in and is helping her make better decisions for her future. She's finishing school and supporting her baby.

Brady, a married Christian, was depressed over a job termination. Unable to find work and feeling unsatisfied with his life, he began spending time at a local fitness center. Returning the advances of a female patron led to an affair. His wife found out, took the kids, and moved out.

Brady may not have had a choice regarding his job situation. He did, however, choose to be unfaithful to his wife. By accepting responsibility for his actions, he has taken a step toward family reconciliation.

For a long time, I excused my actions by blaming my circumstances and others. It was easy to justify my attraction to men because of my father's lack of love or to excuse my anger toward my husband's intimate gestures because I had been raped.

Sinful cycles pass down from generation to generation. (Look up Exodus 34:7 and Numbers 14:18.) We can experience God's forgiveness and restoration through Jesus by repenting (turning away from) our sinful thoughts and behavior. According to 2 Corinthians 5:21, "God made him who had no sin to be sin for us, so that in him we might become the righteousness of God."

Sin, even when forgiven, may have consequences that we can't change. However, through Christ, we have the hope that our children will be free from its influence. Psalm 112:2 gives us a promise that the generations of the upright—the righteous—will be blessed!

As Christians we now have a good example to model our lives after: Jesus. By inviting him to be our Lord, we invite the work of the Holy Spirit to reveal any way we are not pleasing to him.

Remember, God provided the remedy for our guilt and sin. God's forgiveness coupled with a repentant attitude can produce life-changing results. True peace comes from being cleansed through repentance by God's grace and forgiveness.

Reflections

What sinful attitudes or actions are the hardest for you to change?

_____

_____

_____

_____

_____

How have you justified or excused your sinful attitudes and actions?

_____

_____

_____

_____

_____

Journaling Exercise Four

Read Galatians, chapter five, then begin this exercise.

Reflect on verses 19 through 21. What categories of the sinful nature do you identify with?

_____

_____

_____

_____

For each sinful attitude or behavior, ask God to show how it has affected you or your relationships. Write down what is revealed to you.

_____

_____

_____

_____

Determine to take responsibility and resolve to change. Make a commitment, in the strength of God, to sin no more in that way. Write your prayer:

_____

_____

_____

God has made promises on forgiveness. Select two of the following verses that especially touch you and describe what they mean to you.

> *"Blessed is he*
> *whose transgressions are forgiven,*
> *whose sins are covered.*
> *Blessed is the man*
> *whose sin the Lord does not count against him."*
> (Ps. 32:1, 2)

_____

_____

❖ ❖ ❖

> *"When we were overwhelmed by sins,*
> *you forgave our transgressions."* (Ps. 65:3)

_____

_____

❖ ❖ ❖

> *"Praise the Lord ...*
> *who forgives all your sins*
> *and heals all your diseases,*
> *who redeems your life from the pit*
> *and crowns you with love and*
> *compassion ..."* (Ps. 103:2–4)

_____

_____

*"... as far as the east is from the west,
so far has he removed our
transgressions from us."* (Ps. 103:12)

_____

_____

❖ ❖ ❖

*"... 'Though your sins are like scarlet,
they shall be as white as snow;
though they are red as crimson,
they shall be like wool."* (Isa. 1:18)

_____

_____

❖ ❖ ❖

"... 'your guilt is taken away and your sin atoned for.'"
(Isa. 6:7)

_____

_____

❖ ❖ ❖

*"'I have swept away your offenses like a cloud,
your sins like the morning mist'..."* (Isa. 44:22)

_____

_____

❖ ❖ ❖

*"But he was pierced for our transgressions,
he was crushed for our iniquities;*

*the punishment that brought us peace was upon him,
and by his wounds we are healed."* (Isa. 53:5)

❖ ❖ ❖

*"… 'so that you may know the Son of Man
has authority on earth to forgive sins'…"* (Matt. 9:6)

❖ ❖ ❖

"…'Friend, your sins are forgiven'." (Luke 5:20)

❖ ❖ ❖

*"Jesus said, 'Father, forgive them,
for they do not know what they are doing'."* (Luke 23:34)

❖ ❖ ❖

*"In him we have redemption through his blood,
the forgiveness of sins . . ."* (Eph. 1:7)

"For he has rescued us from the dominion of darkness
and brought us into the kingdom of the Son he loves,
in whom we have redemption,
the forgiveness of sins." (Col. 1:13, 14)

❖   ❖   ❖

"And the prayer offered in faith
will make the sick person well;
the Lord will raise him up. If he has sinned,
he will be forgiven. Therefore confess your sins to each
other and pray for each other so that you may be healed."
(James 5:15, 16)

❖   ❖   ❖

"If we confess our sins, he is faithful and just
and will forgive us our sins
and purify us from all unrighteousness." (1 John 1:9)

❖   ❖   ❖

"...Your sins have been forgiven on account of his name."
(1 John 2:12)

Prayer

Have mercy on me, O God,
according to your unfailing love;
according to your great compassion
blot out my transgressions.
Wash away all my iniquity
and cleanse me from my sin
(Ps. 51:1, 2)

Ask God for forgiveness. Pray the following prayer out loud.

Father, you have known my heart all along and never stopped loving me, even when I sinned. Thank you for showing me how (name each sin) *has kept me from being closer to you. Please forgive me for* (name each sin) *and set me free from my sin and guilt, according to your Word.*

Is there anything you would like to add to your prayer?

_____

_____

_____

_____

_____

_____

_____

Accept his forgiveness.

Write out today's date, then write: "I accept your forgiveness, mercy, and love."

_____

_____

_____

_____

_____

_____

Reread Galatians 5:1: "It is for freedom that Christ has set us free. Stand firm, then, and do not let yourselves be burdened again by a yoke of slavery."

Journal your praise and thank him for his faithfulness.

_____

_____

_____

_____

_____

_____

_____

_____

_____

_____

_____

_____

_____

_____

_____

_____

Praise the Lord, O my soul,
and forget not all his benefits—
who forgives all your sins
and heals all your diseases,
who redeems your life from the pit
and crowns you with love and compassion.
—Psalm 103:2–4

Surrender

At the close of many church meetings, the preacher petitions the congregation with Jesus' invitation, "'Come unto me, all you who are weary and burdened, and I will give you rest. Take my yoke upon you and learn from me, for I am gentle and humble in heart, and you will find rest for your souls'" (Matt. 11:28, 29). The preacher then asks, "Won't you come to the altar and just 'give it to Jesus'?" The people march forward, pray a few moments, and go home to find they took "it" with them.

This reminds me of when my toddlers placed inedible and undesirable things in their mouths. We called it "yuck." I'd coax, "Give mommy the yuck, honey," requesting dirt, snails, or whatever to be spit out in my hand. If the yuck came out, we'd applaud and praise with relief. But sometimes the yuck had been swallowed. In that case, no matter how much I coaxed or commanded, a simple spit in the hand wasn't ample effort to expel the yuck. The only way the bad stuff was going to come out was by emptying the stomach.

Giving our problems to Jesus is similar. A simple word or two usually won't do it. I find it requires an emptying of

69

self-will and self-protection. This rarely happens voluntarily and usually happens when crisis has us at the edge of our human abilities. The "coming" must be accompanied with a sincere motivation and desire to be rid of whatever our yuck is. In fact, we must want Jesus more than anything else.

Jesus is asking for surrender—an attitude of brokenness and an abandonment to God—demonstrated through our willingness to

- ◆ trust in him and the truth of his Word
- ◆ recognize our weariness (denied secrets)
- ◆ realize our burden (unrepented sins)
- ◆ surrender our weariness and burdens to his rest

Neglecting our relationship with Jesus—not "coming unto Him"—reveals our attempt to live life apart from God and his Word. I frequently see those in counseling who act like God is there to rubber stamp their plans and whose prayers are reduced to letting God in on the plans.

David wrote Psalm 51 in brokenness and repentance after committing adultery with Bathsheba and being confronted by Nathan. In verse 17 he writes,

> "The sacrifices of God are a broken spirit;
> a broken and contrite heart,
> O God, you will not despise."

David responded so openly only after failing at his own strong-willed attempts to remedy his denial and deceitfulness.

We may call Jesus our Savior but not allow him lordship over our lives. How many of our prayers sincerely ask God to break our self-will and are then willing to allow God to do so? Not all Christians will risk exchanging their own ways for his, even when they say they want to. They have not learned how to come to God with their problems.

The bottom line is that brokenness can be blocked because we are bruised or braced. Many of us must face these personality characteristics when we want to surrender to God but don't know how.

The Bruised

Bruised people look at surrender and respond, "I have been broken all my life. What does God want from me now? Haven't I been through enough?" Just when they think they see light at the end of the tunnel, here comes the freight train!

For those who find themselves always running but never getting anywhere, surrender is confusing and over-whelming. Because they live in a perpetual state of need, always on the brink of crisis, they end up asking what more God could possibly want them to do. And that is their problem. God doesn't want them to do anything. He wants them to let him do something! He wants them to move their focus from their needs to him.

During one support group meeting, we shared past secrets and sins and brought them to the Lord in prayer. One young woman remained reserved and distant. We encouraged her to let God have the yuck of her life.

"I don't like to pray out loud," she said.

71

We said we would pray with her silently. She refused. We encouraged her to tag along on our prayers. She refused.

Perplexed, I did something I had never done before. I pulled a chair into the middle of the group and I confronted her resistance by directly challenging her to sit on the chair and let us pray for her. Now crying, she refused even our prayers. Why wouldn't she respond? The truth was that she wasn't ready. She simply chose to embrace her dilemma rather than offer it to God.

I equate the bruised person with the invalid man by the pool of Bethesda in John's Gospel (John 5:8). He'd been a victim of his circumstance for so long that when Jesus asked him if he wanted to be well, the man began rehearsing his problem. Jesus already knew the problem. All the man needed to do was take his focus off himself and place it onto Jesus.

Jesus then commanded the invalid to pick up his mat and walk. The man picked up his mat and walked. He was cured! Later, when Jesus found the man, he told him, "… you are well again. Stop sinning or something worse may happen to you" (John 5:14). The reference to the man's sin raised a question for me. What sin was Jesus referring to? Jesus' comment was caution against any temptation the man might have to live his life by his own standards. Now that Jesus had healed him, a greater dimension of relationship was expected. Jesus considered anything less than that to be a sin.

Many people are camped out by their own pools of despair and Jesus' invitation to surrender will evoke excuses.

How have you reflected a bruised character?

_____

_____

_____

_____

_____

The Braced

Braced people look at surrender as a sign of weakness. They have just completed a fifteen-week self defense course, have their lives in neat little packages, and along comes the "invitation" to give it all up! "You must be kidding! I have worked darn hard to get where I am, and no one is going to take it from me again." "Only the strong survive" is their motto. Even advertising reinforces *we* can remedy every problem from loose dentures and high mortgages to runaway children and aging parents.

Braced people are always in control. Painful emotions are enemies so braced people escape feelings through behaviors like overeating, oversleeping, overworking, use of pornography, alcohol, drugs, or attempted suicide. Sometimes they hide their fear behind locks, security buildings, police dogs, whistles, or self-defense classes. Or maybe they hide their hurt behind verbal abuse, assault, pride, or procrastination.

After a telephone screening with Samantha, I invited her to attend our support group. During the meeting, her previously congenial personality changed. She didn't like the way we ran our group. She had something negative to say about everyone and everything. She thought I was a poor excuse for a group facilitator. Her resistance to conform to the group superseded her need to be there, and consequently she saw little change in her life during our time together.

Mark's Gospel story about a rich young man gives another illustration. "Jesus looked at him and loved him. ... 'Go, sell everything you have and give to the poor, and you will have treasure in heaven. Then come, follow me.' At this the man's face fell. He went away sad, because he had great wealth" (Mark 10:21–23). Jesus' concern wasn't the man's wealth, but the man's heart, which placed wealth above his relationship with Jesus. Just like this rich man, braced people hang onto something they believe they need more than they need Jesus.

New Testament examples of the Pharisees and their relationship to God reveal attitudes and actions that were braced and resistant to God. They thought they had all the answers and missed the true answer—Jesus. We can learn from them about the fruitlessness of their unteachableness.

In what ways do you reflect a braced character?

_____

_____

_____

_____

_____

Surrender

Alice was the youngest of three sisters, all of whom were molested as children by their stepfather. As a result, young Alice decided she couldn't trust her mother to protect her. The problem today is that her mother is old and in poor health. Alice is going to visit her and wants to try to work things out, but there is something frightful blocking her. She has remembered that, as a child, she made herself a secret promise, that she would never trust her mother again. And she has never been close to her mother. She knows she must let go of that promise in order to have a relationship with her mother.

Jessica was undisciplined and disruptive in my Sunday School class. I was determined to take control of my class and her. So with patience, kindness, goodness, and gentleness I tried to give her lots of special attention.

I hugged her, talked to her, held her in my lap. I reached to tickle her just above the knee when suddenly she pushed my hand away and pulled her dress down over her knees. With a confident tone of voice, Jessica said, "My uncle molested me. He is in jail now, and I never have to see him again." With that, she jumped out of my lap and began her usual disruptive activities. Jessica, at age five, had made a promise to herself that no one would control her again.

These decisions Alice and Jessica made in childhood can affect their relationship with God and others. Resistance to intimacy and relationships is fortified by promises we made in order to survive. Today, if we want to grow in our relationships, we can no longer afford to keep these promises. Explore those decisions, or promises, that block the freedom Christ gave you.

What situations changed your thinking about trusting people or God?

_____

_____

_____

_____

_____

Jesus wants our stability, security, and significance to be in him. The secret to true happiness and peace is loving God with our whole heart, mind, soul, and strength. Jesus asks, "Come unto me." The bruised say, "I can't"; the braced say, "I won't." But they are saying the same thing. They don't trust Jesus, and they don't trust him because they don't know him.

During a support group meeting, we talked about Lazarus and how God wanted to remove our grave clothes and give us a new identity, too. One woman looked down with tears in her eyes and said, "That is so frightening to me. If all the old clothes were gone, who would I be?" I told her I couldn't give her an exact answer, but that I could promise she wouldn't be the same.

The beginning of the breaking point came for me when I became sick and tired of *trying* to be a Christian.

But that wasn't enough. I then had to be sick and tired of being sick and tired. To put all my trust into Jesus was not nearly as frightening as spending the rest of my life being chased by my past and my fears. My hour of desperation motivated me and I "came unto him."

I reached out and finally talked about how I felt and what was going on in my mind and my heart. I asked for prayer and help. I cried before God in utter brokenness with sincere confession of my secrets and repentance of my sins. Many times friends held my hand and interceded in prayer for me, too. For me, surrender contained a flood of tears that extinguished a consuming fire of guilt. For the first time as a Christian, I felt new, and I knew God was real.

I have learned to come often to the feet of Jesus with my problems. Then I crawl up into his lap and let him hold me. I can do that now because I'm free to let him love me and I choose my relationship with him over everything else. David says it sweetly in Psalm 34:8, "Taste and see that the Lord is good; blessed is the man who takes refuge in him."

Scripture gives us many examples of how people changed after being with Jesus. I love the promise at the close of Matthew 14:35–36, "And when the men of that place recognized Jesus, they sent word to all the surrounding country. People brought all their sick to him and begged him to let the sick just touch the edge of his cloak, and all who touched him were healed." When we recognize Jesus, we touch him, and we are healed.

Surrender to the Lord requires being real. Oswald Chambers says in *My Utmost for His Highest* that "to every degree in which we are not real, we will dispute rather than come."[1] When someone runs away from Jesus or runs to anything or anyone but Jesus, their actions indicate they don't trust him. And if they aren't trusting in him, they are trusting in something else. What is it?

Reflections

To what emotional or physical place do you run when crises come?

_____

_____

_____

_____

In what way do you neglect your relationship with Jesus?

_____

_____

_____

_____

Prayer

Ask God to reveal any areas of resistance you may have so that you may fully "come unto him." What does God show you about your resistance and mistrust? Write your prayer, confessing what he has shown you.

_____

_____

_____

_____

We must find the balance between having no control in our lives and having too much control. God doesn't want us to be bruised doormats or braced pillars. He wants us to be balanced, using emotions to express our feelings, using our minds to think with, and using God-given wisdom and discernment. Christ paid for our freedom instantly, but Christian maturity is a process we grow into every day.

I once saw a cartoon that dealt with this. A perplexed and bewildered man stands at the altar for prayer. On one side is an evangelist praying, "God, help him to let go . . . Oh, God, help him to let go." But on the other side is another evangelist praying, "Oh God, help him to hang on . . . Oh, God, help him to hang on."

That is what I am saying, too! We must help the bruised to hang on and teach the braced to let go. We must learn to surrender our struggles while hanging on to God's Word by faith.

F - forsaking
A - all
I - I
T - take
H - Him

Yielding

Teach me, Jesus,
how to pray
more like you,
have your way.
Create the words
within my heart,
so from my lips
they do impart.
Teach me in
the silent hour,
to wait upon
your strength and power.
Mold my life
like yielding clay
in your footsteps
every day.
Jesus Christ,
ever so sweet,
with nail scarred
hands and feet,
I bury old self
with you this day
and resurrect
in power, *your* way.

—Yvonne Martinez

Journaling Exercise Five

Pray and ask for God's wisdom in your life. (Read James 1:5.) Then review your journal from the past few weeks. Because of past experiences, what promises have you made to yourself that keep you from intimacy in relationships, especially in relationship with God?

_____

_____

_____

_____

_____

_____

How have these promises hindered your relationships?

_____

_____

_____

_____

What promises do you need to let go of?

_____

_____

_____

_____

81

What promises do you need to hang on to?

_____

_____

_____

_____

Are you ready to relinquish to God your self-protective promises? Write out your prayer:

_____

_____

_____

_____

_____

_____

_____

_____

_____

_____

_____

"… 'Come!' Whoever is thirsty, let him come; and whoever wishes, let him take the free gift of the water of life."
—Revelation 22:17

Understanding Forgiveness

Forgiveness is a fruit of surrender. Those who surrender their hearts to God choose to forgive, not because they should, but because they want to.

God provides forgiveness for people who were destined to fail but who chose to return to God. In the Old Testament, sin was forgiven through sacrificial offerings. Then God sent his son, Jesus, who for all time is the sacrifice for our sins. It is through Jesus we have forgiveness, and because we have been forgiven we can share forgiveness with others.

In forgiving, we release our judgment or desire for revenge. Three aspects of forgiveness are:

1. Giving forgiveness to those who have offended us.

2. Asking forgiveness for our offenses.

3. Receiving forgiveness for our offenses.

Inpatient hospital programs advertise "Forgiveness Therapy" and an employee from a major corporation recently told me it had scheduled "Personal Enrichment" seminars (which included the topic of forgiveness) to increase self-esteem and productivity of employees. These programs are finding out what God has told us all along—there is a connection between forgiveness and good mental health.

We don't read too far into God's Word without instruction about God's forgiveness or our forgiving others. In fact, *Strong's Exhaustive Concordance of the Bible* lists 102 verses that use the words *forgive, forgiven,* or *forgiveness.*[1] What do the following verses say about forgiveness? Look them up and jot down your thoughts.

Matthew 6:14, 15 _____

Matthew 9:2 _____

Mark 2:7 _____

Mark 11:25, 26 _____

Luke 6:37_____

Luke 11:4 _____

Luke 17:3 _____

Ephesians 4:32 _____

In Matthew 18:21–35, Jesus tells us a parable about a master who cancels a great debt owed by his servant. The servant, in turn, refuses mercy to his debtor. When the master learns about this, he becomes angry and turns the servant over to be tortured until he pays back all he owed. Then Jesus says, "This is how my heavenly Father will treat each of you unless you forgive your brother from your heart" (v. 35).

We have been released from a great eternal judgment for our sins, given a new birth and the promise of eternal life. God wants us to forgive because he has forgiven us. He wants us to show mercy because he has shown us mercy. Having mercy is no longer desiring that others will get what they deserve.

Giving forgiveness to those who have hurt us. When we experience the grace of God's forgiveness we forgive others more freely. We choose to release from our judgment those who have hurt us, and we choose to show mercy toward them. Releasing others from our prideful judgment releases us from the emotional torture unforgiveness produces. Remember, forgiveness releases us. Think of a fish caught on a hook. As the fish struggles and struggles, the hook goes deep into its mouth. Forgiveness cuts the line and sets the fish free to heal.

Giving forgiveness to those who are not sorry. Often we want to set up conditions or see remorse on someone's part before we will forgive them. This really means our forgiveness is conditioned upon the guilty party's repentance. We say, "If you're sorry, I'll forgive you." Jesus says, "I forgive you," and makes us sorry. It is Jesus' forgiveness and mercy that invites our repentance.

Giving forgiveness when you don't feel *like it.* When hurt hasn't been addressed, forgiveness will seem detached from feelings. But forgiveness isn't a choice. It is a scriptural ordinance. The choice involved is whether or not to obey.

It is sort of like looking into a closet that has been cluttered for a long time. You will never enjoy the good feelings that come from having a clean closet while you are still looking at the mess. Just as soon as the closet is clean, though, the feelings come naturally. When you obey God and clean out the clutter of unforgiveness, the good feelings will come.

Giving forgiveness to those who persist in abusing you. Whoever hurts you or abuses you, a Christian, is guilty of sin against God's temple (1 Cor. 3:16; 6:19). Allowing them to continue is not good for them and, of course, not good for you. In every case that Jesus endured or submitted to persecution, it was to bring glory to his Father. Likewise, our submission should bring glory to God or cause others to be drawn to Christ.

When David (1 Samuel) was persecuted and pursued by Saul, he removed himself from the violence until it was safe. On two occasions, David spared Saul's life when he could have killed him in defense. If David had retaliated, he would have been no better than Saul. David was able to leave Saul in God's hands, and God honored David.

Relationships that continue to damage you emotionally or physically need to be handled with the same maturity. You can remove yourself from the abuse and the abuser so you both can seek help. You can pray for the abuser and for healing in both your lives.

Giving forgiveness when you are angry. Being angry is not a sin, but extended hostility, insult, or injury is. Anger has active expressions like yelling and throwing things or hitting people. It also has passive expressions like forget-fulness, procrastination, or apathy. You know anger is a sin when you see its reflection in the lives of others.

Asking forgiveness for our offenses. All the previous Scriptures promise if we confess our sins (and unforgive-ness is a sin), God will forgive us. This forgiveness is guaranteed through Jesus.

When possible, we also need to ask for forgiveness from those directly or indirectly hurt.

Asking for forgiveness when someone refuses to forgive. Your asking for forgiveness is an act of obedience and shows responsibility as well as maturity, but you cannot dictate what the response might be. Another's forgiveness is not your responsibility.

The act of asking for forgiveness releases the one you've wounded. The line from you, the fisher, to the fish has been cut and the fish set free to doctor its wounds.

Receiving forgiveness for our offenses. When we haven't forgiven ourselves, we haven't truly believed God has forgiven us. We continue to punish ourselves for the things Christ died for. This action tells God that his sacrifice of Jesus was not enough to pay for our sins.

We cannot do anything to remedy our sins. Jesus alone can remove them through his atonement. The whole thing has nothing to do with us and has everything to do with him. Receiving forgiveness is accepting God at his Word.

Unforgiveness. I visited a Christian woman. Two years earlier her pastor had raped her during a counseling session. She recently had a nervous breakdown and was hospitalized. When I asked her about forgiveness, she said she would *never* forgive him for what he did. The unforgiveness allowed him to rape her over and over in her mind.

This conversation came to my mind one evening when I opened a can of tomatoes and poured them into a pan while making dinner. I looked into the empty container and saw corrosion on the inside of the can. I checked the outside of the can and found it had been dented. I realized the can and its contents were spoiled.

The Lord showed me that this is how unforgiveness is in our hearts. Our unforgiveness is like acid in a fragile cup. A blow to the outside eats away the quality from the inside and damages the contents.

The forgiver pays a great price and the guilty goes free. This is the example that Christ gave us. He forgave and we go free. There was no other payment for our sin. Unforgiveness will never remedy a wrong. In most cases the emotional or physical damage is either irreparable or irreplaceable. Likewise, we forgive because repayment is impossible and unforgiveness is a death-grip on pain.

Reread Matthew 18:21–35. What great debt have you been released from?

_____

_____

_____

_____

_____

Who is the servant in your life you need to release from your judgment and show mercy to?

_____

_____

_____

_____

_____

Why do you need to forgive, even if the other isn't sorry?

_____

_____

_____

_____

_____

_____

Why do you need to forgive, even if you don't feel like it?

_____

_____

_____

_____

_____

_____

If you're involved in an abusive relationship, what can you do to be both wise and mature?

_____

_____

_____

_____

_____

How is your anger reflected in sinful ways?

_____

_____

_____

_____

_____

Who do you need to ask mercy and forgiveness from?

_____

_____

_____

_____

_____

How will you do this?

_____

_____

_____

_____

What if this person won't forgive you?

_____

_____

_____

_____

In what way do you continue to punish yourself for the things Christ died for?

_____

_____

_____

_____

What do you deny yourself?

_____

_____

_____

_____

In what ways do you withhold forgiving yourself?

_____

_____

_____

_____

Do you believe that God will forgive you if you ask? Why?

_____

_____

_____

_____

The surrendered heart no longer wants the excess baggage of unforgiveness. Forgiveness, then, becomes a welcomed practice. If you find difficulty in forgiving your offender, what would need to happen for you to forgive? Answer by completing this sentence.

I will forgive _____ *if* _____

_____

_____

What did Jesus say in Luke 23:34?

_____

_____

Why do you think Jesus said this?

_____

_____

_____

With Jesus' attitude in mind, prayerfully complete the following sentences.

Giving Forgiveness

Father, I forgive_____ for_____; he (she) did not know what he (she) was doing.

Asking Forgiveness

Father, forgive me for _____; I'm sorry for what I have done.

Father, help me go to _____ and ask for forgiveness. (If this person has died, asking God for his forgiveness is sufficient. It is unbiblical to pray to or try to communicate with anyone who is deceased.)

Receiving Forgiveness

Father, I receive your forgiveness for _____.
Father, I forgive myself for _____.

Conclude this part of the exercise with the following prayer:

Father, I bring to you all my secrets and all my sins and surrender my heart. I will no longer seek for acceptance from anyone but you. I will no longer seek for approval from anyone but you. I will no longer punish myself for those things you have forgiven. I commit my life to loving and serving you. Praise you and thank you.
Amen.

How do you feel now? _____

_____

_____

_____

_____

What Forgiveness Isn't

Sometimes I am asked, "Why, if I have forgiven someone, does it bother me or still hurt? Does it mean I haven't forgiven them?" I try to assure the person that forgiveness is essential to healing. However, the truth is that forgiveness has as many layers as we have hurts, and sometimes the consequences of sin can't be changed with forgiving the offender. Remember, forgiveness releases us from our judgment and allows us to heal.

Forgiveness isn't denying the pain. My family asked me to call on a Christian friend who had been attacked. She told me what had happened, and then said she knew the reason she was still alive. After her attacker had raped her and begun to stab her with a knife, she told him Jesus loved him and he didn't have to do this. With her words, he ran from the house. She called the police, and an ambulance took her to the hospital.

Forgiveness and mercy didn't erase her need for medical attention. The same is true of our emotional wounds. Forgiveness sets us free from the offender, but we may need help in putting our lives back on track.

Forgiveness isn't excusing the crime. Jesus acknowledged the repentant thief hanging on the cross next to him. In his compassion toward the thief, Jesus told him he'd be in paradise that day. But the thief still died for his crime. My husband, Tony, leads our prison ministry. Every service he ministers to men who have been forgiven and set free by Christ, yet who are still serving their sentences. Forgiveness rectifies the spiritual judgment, but it doesn't necessarily absolve from the restitution required according to the law.

Forgiveness isn't reconciliation. Forgiving doesn't mean you will, or can, have close relationships with the ones you forgive.

My father died before I became a Christian. Forgiveness couldn't reconcile our relationship, but I have the peace of knowing I let go of my hurt and anger. Through Christ, I was able to forgive him for his rejection and abandonment.

In the example of David and Saul, it wasn't safe for David to remain close to Saul. David was willing, but Saul's attitude and actions stood in the way of their relationship. If Saul had been willing to change, the story would have had a much different ending.

Forgiveness isn't reconciliation, but it's a beginning.
Today's language would describe David as detaching himself from Saul and establishing boundaries to protect himself. The goal for David, and for us, is to back up, catch our
breath, redesign our plan, and merge back into our lives as
ambassadors of Christ Jesus.

Returning to the fishing metaphor from page 85, we
need to cut the line, remove the hook, and doctor our
wounds. During this process we learn valuable lessons
about where the fisher fishes and what bait to look out for
lest we bite the hook again.

Moving beyond the physical healing involves mercy
and prayerful intercession for the fisher. This will not
guarantee reconciliation with the fisher, but we will swim
along happier because forgiveness *will* guarantee reconciliation with God.

We also need to resolve the question of anger toward
God. It's often easier to forgive someone who didn't know
any better than to forgive God. After all, God is well aware
of the events that happened in our life, and yet, for his
reasons, didn't change them. Just today I had a call from
someone wrestling with the questions: "Where was God
when this happened, and why didn't he stop it?"

There are several books that discuss why God allows
evil, why bad things happen to good people, and what to
do when life is unfair. But, even after reading all the right
books, I still had to personally settle these same questions
for myself.

In the midst of the pain, I couldn't understand God or
what he was doing in my life. Now, in retrospect, I see the

good that came from the bad. I see that life is unfair, but God is fair. I see that I must trust in him no matter what the circumstances look like. I had to ask God to forgive me for my anger and apathy toward him. I have learned to be thankful for my past, for what he allowed.

I Told God I Was Angry

I told God I was angry.
I thought he'd be surprised.
I thought I'd kept hostility
quite cleverly disguised.

I told the Lord I hate him.
I told him that I hurt.
I told him that he isn't fair,
He's treated me like dirt.

I told God I was angry
but I'm the one surprised.
"What I've known all along," he said,
"you've finally realized."

"At last you have admitted
what's really in your heart.
Dishonesty, not anger,
was keeping us apart.

"Even when you hate me
I don't stop loving you.
Before you can receive that love
you must confess what's true.

"In telling me the anger
you genuinely feel,
it loses power over you,
permitting you to heal."

I told God I was sorry
and he's forgiven me.
The truth that I was angry
has finally set me free.

—Jessica Shaver [2]

Reflections

How do you relate to Jessica's poem?

_____

_____

_____

_____

_____

_____

_____

_____

_____

_____

Prayer

If you are angry at God, write him a letter about your feelings. Ask his forgiveness for your anger and apathy toward him. Ask him to show you his love for you.

_____

_____

_____

_____

_____

_____

_____

_____

There is a myth that I believed and is believed by most victims. This myth is:

> One day, if I work real hard at it, I will be whole. When that day comes all my personal problems will be re-solved. Then I will be happy. One day, when I am whole, things will be different ... I won't have problems or fears or worries. Life will be perfect if I can just get through this time.

Some secular therapy and counseling perpetuates this myth by taking you through a maze, a journey inward to find the answers to your problems. The answers will never be found there, and I know people who have been in therapy for thirty years. We don't have the answer, Jesus does. So the answer must be found out of ourselves, in a journey to discover him. That is a life-long process because he will never be known fully this side of heaven.

The myth is also perpetuated by those who say, because you are a Christian, you will have it all now—all health, all healing, all happiness. I believe we have a biblical basis to ask for it, and I believe we can hope and pray for it. I also believe that even if we don't attain perfect health, healing, and happiness here on earth, it doesn't mean we have failed.

The truth is that reconciling your past does not place you in a bubble, protecting you from the influence of a sinful world, but it can give you tools to avoid becoming victimized again. Jesus promises us that one day there will be no more tears, no more pain, no more death, and all things will be made new (Rev. 21:1–5). That promise will be realized in Heaven, when we see Jesus face to face.

"Give, and it will be given to you. A good measure, pressed down, shaken together and running over, will be poured into your lap. For with the measure you use, it will be measured to you."
—Luke 6:38

Recognizing the Enemy

For though we live in the world, we do not wage war as the world does. The weapons we fight with are not the weapons of the world. On the contrary, they have divine power to demolish strongholds. We demolish arguments and every pretension that sets itself up against the knowledge of God, and we take captive every thought to make it obedient to Christ. (2 Cor. 10:3–5)

These verses in 2 Corinthians tell me if we are in a war and we have weapons, we must have an enemy! The warfare is not like the world's wars, rather it is a spiritual war that began when Satan first rebelled against God in the heavens. To ignore this warfare would be a disservice to you and to those I have aimed to help, as would making it the sole solution. We need to be aware and armed but not alarmed!

I was defeated in the world and as a new Christian I was still being defeated. My Christian walk was void of peace, pleasure, or power and plagued with doubt, depression, and disaster. Christ had given me security and authority, I just didn't know about it.

Sometimes I awoke at the stroke of midnight paralyzed by nightmares in which awful things chased me and I had nowhere to run. Other times I heard voices say I was going to die. Even during the most intimate moments with my husband, the face of my rapist or the hands of my molester would taunt me. Because of these fears, I thought I didn't really belong to God. I thought Christians couldn't be tormented by bizarre thoughts and feelings. I doubted my salvation.

I couldn't afford counseling and went to a small church where everyone was perfect. Spiritual warfare drove me to ask questions, read books, and search God's Word to find an answer and a way out. During my most fearful minutes and hours, I learned to rehearse God's Word, sing his praises, and pray. God was faithful when I couldn't feel or hear him. My healing came as a result of learning more about God and who I am in Jesus. My attitudes and behavior changed as I confessed my secrets and my sins and surrendered to his Word. I made a determination to trust God. I am where I am today solely because of Jesus' faithfulness in love, grace, and power to heal and set free.

Read Ephesians 1:18–23 for yourself in context with the entire first chapter of Ephesians to realize the full impact of what is being said to us.

Personalize these Scriptures in the following prayer.

Prayer

Father, God, I ask for your awakening in my mind that I might know the hope to which you have called me, the riches of your glorious inheritance in me, and your incomparably great power for me who believes. That power is like the working of your mighty strength, which you exerted in Christ when you raised him from the dead and seated him at your right hand in the heavenly realms, far above all rule and authority, power and dominion, and every title that can be given, not only in the present age but also in the one to come. And you placed all things under Jesus' feet and appointed him to be head over everything for the church (me), which is Jesus' body, the fullness of him who fills everything in every way.

Victims are victims because they didn't learn how, or weren't able, to fight and win against the enemies in their world. As Christians, they can still be victims—spiritual victims—not knowing who they are in Christ or what choices they have.

To blame everything on the devil eliminates the need to control our fleshly desires or repent from sinful behaviors. We also live in a world that pulls against our godly morals and values. The warfare is real and persistent. We have a genuine enemy who desires to see us fall and fail.

Jesus was confronted by Satan. Why would we think we would be immune to the adversity? Satan can't get us to hell but he can put a little hell in our lives. God's Word makes us aware of our warfare.

What does Job 1:12 say about Satan's ability to afflict the righteous?

_____

_____

_____

_____

_____

What does Acts 26:18 say about sinners who have been under Satan's authority?

_____

_____

_____

What does Ephesians 6:12 warn us about?

_____

_____

_____

The Bible says our enemy is called by different names. List the names you find in the following verses.

Revelation 12:10 _____

1 Peter 5:8 _____

Revelation 9:11 _____

Matthew 4:1 _____

2 Corinthians 4:4 _____

John 8:44 _____

Isaiah 14:12 _____

Ephesians 2:2 _____

John 14:30 _____

Ephesians 6:12 _____

Acts 5:3 _____

Matthew 4:3 _____

Matthew 13:19 _____

This partial list of names reveals characteristics of his personality. They help us identify his strategy, which aims to attack the very core of our relationship with God.

Our Enemy's Strategy

Devourer

What does 1 Peter 5:8 say about the devil as a devourer?

_____

_____

A lion plays by his own rules. Just as a lion is king of the forest, Satan is prince of this world (John 14:30). There is no love, no mercy, no forgiveness in his game.

A lion stalks his prey. Satan cannot be everywhere and doesn't know everything. However, he has been around for a long time and sees us and the world from a different vantage point. He watches and waits for a precise time.

A lion attacks during an unguarded moment. He finds us off guard when there is trauma and our attention is distracted; sinful rebellion, when we know something is wrong and do it anyway; or foolishness, like playing with the occult or any number of things we do, thinking we are above harm. He attacks by placing a wedge between Christians and their faith. Satan's goal is to neutralize Christians' effectiveness and destroy their influence.

A lion defends his territory. His claim is stacked with doubt, deception, and delusion. His progressive success creates a stronghold, an area of predominance.

Liar

What does John 8:44 say about the devil as a liar?

_____

_____

Satan's game plan hasn't changed since his encounter with Adam and Eve in the Garden of Eden (read Genesis 3). We can dissect their conversation to learn a little more about his strategy.

A liar plants doubt. Satan's first move against Eve was to plant skepticism or disbelief in her mind about the character of God.

A liar plants deception. Satan used deliberate conceal-ment or misrepresentation, and Eve believed the lie.

A liar plants delusion. Satan's rebellion and self-will was now evident in Eve. Her belief rendered her unable to detect falsehood or make sound judgment.

Our Victory

What does Colossians 2:15 say about our victory?

_____

_____

How did Satan fail in his attempt to overthrow God? (Isaiah 14:12–15).

_____

_____

How did Jesus foil Satan's attempts to overthrow him? (Hebrews 2:14, 1 John 3:8, Matthew 28:18).

_____

_____

Why will Satan fail in his attempt to overthrow us? (Acts 1:8, Ephesians 1:18–23, Colossians 1:13).

_____

_____

Why is Satan's rebellion against God intensified? (Revelation 20:10)

_____

_____

_____

Write out Colossians 1:21–23.

_____

_____

_____

_____

_____

_____

_____

_____

_____

_____

_____

_____

_____

What do these verses tell you about your security in Jesus?

_____

_____

_____

_____

_____

Write out John 1:12, 13.

_____

_____

_____

_____

_____

_____

What do these verses tell you about your son- or daughter-ship?

_____

_____

Write out Luke 10:19.

_____

_____

_____

_____

_____

What assurance does this verse tell you about your call to service?

_____

_____

Write out Revelation 3:21.

_____

_____

_____

_____

_____

What does this verse tell you about your future?

_____

_____

_____

Our Weapons

Our mind and flesh cannot win against an experienced warrior like Satan, but Jesus can and did. Jesus is both our shield and our arrow.

> Herod could not kill him
> Satan could not seduce him
> Death could not destroy him
> and the Grave could not hold him[1]

Look up and write down the following references to Jesus' blood, name, and Word. Find out for yourself how pure, priceless, powerful, and preserving these weapons are.

His Blood

    Leviticus 17:11 _____

    1 Peter 1:18–20 _____

    Revelation 12:11 _____

    Hebrews 10:10 _____

His Name

    Philippians 2:9 _____

    Isaiah 7:14 _____

    Philippians 2:10 _____

    John 14:6 _____

His Word

    Psalm 12:6 _____

    John 1:1 _____

    Hebrews 4:12 _____

    I Peter 1:23 _____

Our Strategy

These powerful tools sealed in envelopes of prayer are the weapons of our warfare.

Satan fears detection. His loss comes when his defense, built on lies, is shattered by the truth of God's Word. Satan's only ally is the mind of those who don't know who they are in Christ Jesus.

"Finally, be strong in the Lord and in his mighty power. Put on the full armor of God so that you can take your stand against the devil's schemes." (Eph. 6:10–11; read the rest of chapter 6.)

We began our lessons based on God's Word and we end them based on God's Word. The more we learn about ourselves, our world, and our enemy, the more driven we should be to learn about our God. Our circle of hope is forever centered on God's Word manifested through Jesus Christ.

Read 2 Corinthians 10:3–5. Personalize these Scriptures through the following prayer.

Prayer

Father, though we live in the world, we do not wage war as the world does. You have given Jesus' blood, his name, and your Word, the Armor and Prayer—our mighty weapons. These weapons have divine power, your power, to demolish any stronghold of doubt, deception, or delusion.

Right now, I use these weapons to demolish these arguments and pretensions. (Name the doubt[s] or deception[s] you previously accepted.)

_____

_____

_____

_____

_____

_____

_____

These have set themselves against you and I confess I once accepted them. I take those thoughts captive by repenting and renouncing their validity and make them obedient to Christ by submitting to the truth in your Word.

(List Scripture verses that best reflect your affirmation.)

_____

_____

_____

_____

_____

_____

I believe I have your Holy Spirit that promises to guide me into all truth. I give you praise, honor, and glory with a thankful heart. Amen.

After completing this exercise, reread it aloud as a prayer to God.

Who Are You in Christ?

Answer who or how you are by naming the main theme of each of the following Scriptures.

Romans 8:16 _____ A child of God _____

1 Corinthians 6:11 ___ Sanctified _____

Psalm 107:2 _____

Colossians 1:13,14 _____

Ephesians 2:8 _____

Romans 5:1 _____

2 Corinthians 5:17 _____

2 Peter 1:4 _____

Galatians 3:13 _____

Colossians 3:13 _____

Romans 8:14 _____

Psalm 91:11 _____

Philippians 4:19 _____

1 Peter 5:7 _____

Ephesians 6:10 _____

Philippians 4:13 _____

Romans 8:17 _____

Deuteronomy 28:12 _____

Deuteronomy 28:6 _____

1 John 5:11, 12 _____

Ephesians 1:3 _____

1 Peter 2:24 _____

Luke 10:19 _____

Deuteronomy 28:13 _____

Romans 8:37 _____

Matthew 16:19 _____

Revelation 12:11 _____

1 John 4:4 _____

2 Corinthians 4:18 _____

2 Corinthians 5:7 _____

Romans 12:1, 2 _____

1 Corinthians 3:9 _____

Ephesians 5:1 _____

Matthew 5:14 _____

Colossians 3:12; Romans 8:33 _____

Ephesians 1:13 _____

2 Corinthians 5:18 _____

2 Corinthians 5:20 _____

2 Corinthians 3:18 _____

Colossians 2:10 _____

Revelation 21:7 _____

Handling Our Thoughts

Sometimes even when we believe and understand our new life in Christ, thoughts come into our mind causing us to doubt or fear. They seem to be like a slide presentation, one after another. If the thoughts are accepted or discounted, they usually vanish. The ones that linger and consume our productivity demand our attention. They are usually thoughts that strike a vulnerable or unresolved emotional area.

Being confronted by our thoughts and feelings isn't necessarily negative. The source can be promptings from the Holy Spirit leading us into truth, self-talk (the mind rehearsing conversations or events), or the enemy's attempt to throw us off course. When the thought is persistent and you don't know the source or can't resolve it, challenge it with the following process.

Is this condemnation or conviction? Condemnation is from the enemy. It produces guilt with spiritual death as a goal. It overshadows and lurks over sin, constantly bringing it to life, never letting it die.

Conviction is from the Holy Spirit. It produces guilt with holiness as a goal. It also overshadows sin but wants to bring it to death so Christ can live and reign.

Is this temptation or a test? Temptation is from the enemy. Its goal is sin and separation from God. The attractive package contains handcuffs. If you indulge, the attraction will turn to distraction and condemnation will scream accusations.

A test is from God. Its goal is Christian character, and it draws us closer to God. Tests can be a refining influence or chastisement. They don't usually feel good but ultimately work for our good.

Resolution. If thoughts are from an area previously taken to God, you know that Christ has forgiven you and you have forgiven others, then stand firm, rejecting the accusation.

If you are not sure, pray about it immediately. Resolve the guilt by taking responsibility for the sin and ask for forgiveness. If it is not your sin, place responsibility where it belongs and forgive. Then take your stand and thank Jesus. Write the date and time in your journal as a reminder that Jesus took care of this for you today.

If you are being invited to bite into a new sin or to repeat a previous one, refuse and take a stand against it. This requires discipline and practice. Being tempted does not mean you are sinning. Remember, Jesus was tempted.

If you don't exercise your position and fire your weapons, you will find yourself caught in the enemy's scheme. Pray about your circumstances *immediately.* Repent and ask for forgiveness. Learn from your mistake and don't take off the Armor again!

If you are in the midst of a test, be steadfast in praise and prayer. Don't be tempted to give up or to think God has given up on you. I read a greeting card that said, "Sometimes God calms the storm; other times he comforts the child while the storm rages." Either way, God *will* see you through it. He keeps his promises.

Reflections

If you are experiencing thoughts and feelings that are disturbing your prayer life or productivity, write a detailed description of what's going on. As you write, ask God to show you the source (conviction, condemnation, temptation, test).

_____

_____

_____

_____

_____

Apply the teaching to your situation. How will you take a stand?

_____

_____

_____

_____

Prayer

Thank God, in your prayer, for what he has shown you about your victory in Jesus.

_____

_____

_____

_____

_____

_____

The Lord is faithful, and he will strengthen and protect you from the evil one.
—2 Thessalonians 3:3

The Victor

The End Is a Beginning

The end of this book is the beginning of new hope as well as new challenges. It represents a sunset that says good-bye to yesterday and a sunrise that says hello to tomorrow.

To know where tomorrow leads, you need to reflect on your yesterday and the progress you have made since the study began. Evaluating your progress will help you determine if your discernment and perception of your needs is accurate.

Reflections

Completing the following sentences will help you to see the influence God and the study has had on you.

What new ways did you learn to cope with your problems?

_____

_____

_____

♦ The most important tool I learned was _____

♦ The most significant way I feel I have grown is

♦ Since the study began, God has showed me

In what way do you accept your past and no longer dwell on painful memories?

_____

_____

_____

_____

_____

_____

_____

- When confronted with painful memories in the future I will _____

  _____

  _____

  _____

- When I feel discouraged I know I can _____

  _____

  _____

  _____

  _____

♦ I now trust God with_____

_____

_____

_____

_____

Do you believe God has a purpose for you? How will you seek his direction?

_____

_____

_____

_____

_____

_____

_____

♦ I now have hope for myself because I know

_____

_____

_____

_____

_____

◆ I can use this hope to help others through

_____

_____

_____

_____

_____

◆ God wants to use the healed areas in my life by

_____

_____

_____

_____

_____

◆ I am seeking his direction for

_____

_____

_____

_____

_____

In evaluating where you are now, it is just as important to be truthful and acknowledge any areas that need further healing. Finish these sentences.

Areas I haven't been able to surrender to God are

_____

_____

_____

_____

I still need to forgive _____

_____

_____

_____

_____

What are your plans for these areas that still need God's healing power? _____

_____

_____

_____

_____

For the area(s) that still needs healing, I feel God wants me to _____

_____

_____

_____

Prayer

Review specific lessons from the workbook that relate to your problems. Ask God to help you be willing to surrender them to him.

Pray for yourself by taking any unresolved area to God through prayer. Write out your prayer:

If this book has opened up awareness and feelings that need further healing, call your local church or Christian bookstore for a list of other ministries, support groups, Bible studies, or in-home fellowships where you can participate in continued discipleship.

If you made a lot of progress but still need more healing, give yourself permission to rest. Take a break from working on things. Remember the principles you have been taught, and pray you will have courage to seek after God for your future. If you remain open to the Holy Spirit, your awareness of additional needs will surface. At that point you can seek counseling or a support group.

A New Beginning

If you have made significant progress and experienced healing, the end of this study will be the beginning of new hope. It will be like a diploma on graduation day. Be thankful for the study, but accept that it is over and look forward to a new season in your life.

I thank God you had the courage and persistence to complete the exercises in this book and genuinely pray that through them, he has touched your life.

Conclude your study by completing this sentence: The most important thing I want to thank God for is

_____

_____

_____

_____

_____

_____

_____

Thanks be to God! He gives us the victory
through our Lord Jesus Christ.
—1 Corinthians 15:57

Notes

Healing Ingredient Four
1. Oswald Chambers, *My Utmost for His Highest* (Westwood, NJ: Barbour and Company, Inc.), p. 170.

Healing Ingredient Five
1. James Strong, *Strong's Exhaustive Concordance of the Bible* (Nashville, TN: Crusade Bible Publishers, Inc.).
2. Jessica Shaver; *I Told God I Was Angry.*

Healing Ingredient Six
1. Author unknown.